Books by
TJ

Poetry

The Desires of a Woman:
Poems Celebrating Womanhood

In Love:
Poems Celebrating the Essence of Love

Novels

Sorority Sisters
Hand-me-down Heartache
The Night Before Thirty
Just My Luck

In Love: Poems Celebrating the Essence of Love

Tajuana "TJ" Butler-Jackson

Presents

In
LOVE

Poems Celebrating the Essence of Love

Gold Series

Lavelle Publishing
Indianapolis, IN 46236

Published by Lavelle Publishing

First Printing November 2016

In Love: Poems Celebrating the Essence of Love
Lavelle Publishing Gold Series
Copyright © 2016 by Tajuana Jackson

All Rights Reserved
SBN-10: 0-9659254-7-1
ISBN-13: 978-0-9659254-7-1

Printed in the United States of America
Editors: Marita Ward, Robert Jackson
Designed by: Tajuana Jackson

In Love: Poems Celebrating the Essence of Love is available at special discounts when purchased in bulk for premiums and sales promotions as well as for fundraising or educational purposes. For details contact publicist@tjbutler.com.

Table of Contents

Preface

Growing up, I don't recall giving a lot of thought to the idea of love. I just knew that I loved my parents and my sisters. I loved my grandparents and my aunts and my cousins. My love for these people has been a truth that has never changed. I have only ever struggled with three other loves in my life. I struggled with the ability to love myself. I didn't think I had the capability of loving a man enough to settle down. The love that I was most challenged with was developing an authentic love for God. What made love so challenging for me is that I never quite understood what it was, not fully anyway. Don't get me wrong; I come from a huge, beautiful extended family that is sharing and caring, which is probably why I had no problem understanding that I loved them and that they loved me. However, in the other areas, it took me a while to learn and understand the true meaning or function of agape love.

I was aware that Jesus died for my sins because he loved me, however, I didn't fully comprehended what that meant. Everybody that I knew still considered themselves sinners, even though they were saved by grace. I felt guilty every time I sinned according to the Ten Commandments. There were some things I did that I thought were unforgivable. For example, I tolerated tremendous stress and turmoil during the completion of a project. I had worked diligently for several long days and nights, for months, to complete this huge undertaking. What was supposed to be a happy time turned out to be frustrating. I had endured the drama of dealing with personalities that I had never been forced to work with in such close proximity, including people who were malicious, unloyal, and disrespectful. When it was all over I was angry and fatigued. At the conclusion of the event, in front of a large audience, I thanked everyone except God. In hindsight, I felt like I had been blatantly disrespectful. As a result, I rationalized that I had let God down in a major way and that He was angry. Surely, He couldn't love me any more.

Concerning men, although I wanted to eventually commit, I didn't trust them. I found myself drawn to men who were too clingy and ready to settle down immediately, or who were self-centered and emotionally unavailable. Looking back, it makes sense why I would find myself involved with those kinds of men, because it gave me an excuse to exit the relationship. When either I felt like things were getting too serious or felt like the guy didn't count me a priority, I moved on with no regard.

Regarding myself, how could I have properly loved myself when I didn't even understand who I was. I was born the middle child. My oldest sister was a great conversationalist and my youngest sister, was the "baby," and seemed to easily get a pass from being punished when she misbehaved. Because of my position between them, I felt like I wasn't really special or worthy of attention. As my personality developed, it made sense to me to sit back and just try to blend in. As a matter of fact, I spent most of my life shrinking from attention and staying to myself. As a child I found comfort discovering my own space and humming my favorite songs. When I became a bestselling author, I learned to appear confident and comfortable in my skin, but it was during the ten years that I spent most of my time traveling the U. S. as a public speaker and author that I was most lost and unsure of who I really was. I liked a lot of things about myself, but I was critical of my flaws, and I never loved myself enough to choose my needs over the needs of other people.

My journey to gaining a better understanding of true love has been bittersweet. The bitter has been challenging; including me choosing to give my life to Christ, not because of my love for him or His for me, but after having my first anxiety attack. Also, the ridiculously unnecessary arguments that my husband and I found ourselves in during the first part of our relationship. The sweet has been the best experiences I could ever dream of having, including giving birth, getting to the other side of the power struggle and finding real love with my husband. Also, spending intimate time with my parents and siblings, raising three beautiful children, and most important of all, realizing the depth of God's love for me.

When I became a student of the gospel of Jesus Christ, I gained a deeper understanding of agape love. I completely accept that God's love for me is unconditional and that there is nothing I can do bad or good to make him stop loving me. With that understanding firmly planted in my being, I have a new outlook on the way that I see others and myself. I grasp that we all are flawed and in need of a savior. However, it is not only on each of us to receive, appreciate and walk in the truth that our savior loves us so much that he died and was resurrected so we can have abundant life, but also to study to comprehend the magnitude of what that really means for us.

God's sweet love now sustains me, even through the toughest of times. It is what has strengthened my marriage and helped me to be a better parent. It has also helped me to know exactly who I am through Christ. Finding my identity has allowed me to love myself through my flaws. It has helped me, despite anyone's opinion of me, to appreciate my quirks and to be so much more comfortable in my own skin. Today I happily embrace abundant life filled with love, joy and peace.

The poems that I have included in this book are a collection that reflects not only the agape love that I have come to better understand, but also romantic love, family love and self-love. I am excited to share the first book from my upcoming series of poetry books. I pray that they will be a blessing to you and the people around you.

Life is a journey, not one of us is perfect, be we all must strive to be better. Love is a fundamental place to build from. So, no matter our circumstances, let's choose to love our way out, through, beyond, and to.

Yours In Love,
Tajuana "TJ" Butler-Jackson

The Thing About Love

The thing about Love
Is that it was, is, and always will be.

The question is,
Do you truly believe?

Real Love

If somebody would have told me
When I was a little girl
Just what love really meant
Maybe I would have been a better lover

If someone would have just taken the time to tell me
That love is not:
A fairy tale
Floating on a cloud
Living happily ever after
Not being able to stop thinking about the other person
Saying, "No, you hang up," "No, you hang up," over the
phone
Kissing until you can't feel your lips
Your heart racing wildly, uncontrollably
Longing, needing, wanting
Riding off into the sunset with Prince Charming

That love is not:
The grand gesture of kneeling and requesting my hand

Sending me a dozen long stem red roses
Hiding a ring in my champagne glass
Having a band march down the street, playing our favorite song
Taking out a full-page ad in a newspaper
Having a skywriter spell out our love for everyone to see

It is not:
Sweeping me off on a romantic vacation to Europe
Candlelit dinner on the beach
Taking long walks in the fall
Sending a letter asking do you love me? Check yes or no
Filling my living room with balloons
Declaring your love for me on social media
Sending me chocolate candy on Valentine's Day

All those things
Are romantic, beautiful, wonderful
Memorable
Endearing
But they are not Love

If someone would have just taken the time to tell me
That love is not:
Arguing at the top of our lungs
Walking out when I don't get my way
Slamming the door behind me, fuming with anger
Not trusting the others' actions
Not being trustworthy

Being afraid to express or even show how I really feel
Taking advantage of another's weakness
All of those things
Are immature, selfish, wrong
Unacceptable
Misguided
But they are not Love

If somebody would have told me
That love is:
Loving when I don't want to like
Biting my tongue when I wanna go off
Removing the plank from my eye
Instead of focusing on the splinter in his
Nursing the other in sickness
Trusting the process of the power struggle
Not stressing until it's how I think it should be
A simple apology changing the little things
Trusting that God will handle everything

And that it is also:
Not wanting to be apart even after an argument
Not being satisfied until we've both made up
You having my back, me having your back
Appreciating growth
Building a legacy
Deciding to love

Love is a choice,

It is:
What you do through the chaos
It is:
What heals and maintains
What causes the bad to become better

It is:
What gets you through the power struggle

If somebody would have told me
When I was a little girl
Just what love really meant
I still would have wanted it
I just would have been a better lover

What About Love

It's almost like we forgot
or turned away from
or lost trust in
The only thing that maintains
When all else fails

It seems that we stopped believing
or found fault in
or outright excommunicated ourselves from
That which should have been
Held above all others

We thought the answer was
Something different, like
Finding the perfect object for our misguided affection
Getting our education, joining some social organizations
Moving in the right neighborhood, improving our eco-
nomic status
Buying a car, becoming a star
Even if only on Facebook

We must be on some kind of psycho mad trip when
Committing a crime will make you infamous
Being a bitch will get you rich
Cussing and fussing will draw more fans
Nobody seems to care when you steal another woman's
man

All around us we've lost our way and
It's evident in our music, or movies, our video games
Our sitcoms and dramas and reality TV
It's how badly we treat each other and
don't care if anyone is looking

But what we have chosen
Couldn't have been the answer
It couldn't have
How could it be?
If we envy, boast, consistently dishonor and
Keep records of wrong
Are self-seeking and easily angered
Relish in our pride
And delight in evil

So what about love?
Is it an option anymore?
Can we still embody
The patience and kindness love calls for?
Can we still seek to protect,

Not just the physical, but also the mental?
Can we trust and be trusted?
Is there hope?
Do we still hope?
What about perseverance
Can we always preserve?
Can we, will we?
Love

His Kind of
Love

Fred asked many years ago
"What kind of love is this?"
I don't think I really understood back then
But it sounded so good that I closed my eyes
And sang along to the powerful seeming song

Today I know specifically what kind of love it is
And I am in love with this peculiar love
Now I experience, daily, the kind of words
That never meant much to me before
Like sovereignty, liberty and righteousness

And to know that there is nothing that I could do to earn
this love
Nothing I can do to change this love
Nothing I can do to stop this love
Nothing I can do to deserve this love

I freely accept this kind of love
It is the kind of love that can only be given

Once
It can only be given by
One
But it can be experienced by
All

It is
The love of Jesus
The love of my Savior
The love of my God
As only He can give

His word made flesh
Purely out of our need of him
Purely out of his kind of love for us

Love is Contagious

Dedicated to My Daddy

We were daddy's girls
Daddy worked hard
Provided
He left us money for school
Lined up on his dresser

We girls got together
And conspired to tell him we love him
So, one day we did

"Daddy," we said. "We love you."
"Okay," he replied

This went on and then one day
"Daddy," we said. "We love you."
"Daddy loves you too," he replied

We smiled
That was so special to us

This went on and then one day
And now most days
Daddy says, "Daddy loves you."
First

Spread Love

I had a vision of love
And Love lifted me
It was the greatest love of all
That's why
I've learned to respect the power of love

Everybody loves somebody and
I got love on my mind
Do you mind if I put it on your mind
What's love got to do with it?
You ask,
E-v-e-r-y-t-h-i-n-g!

The simple four-letter word
That's got everybody
Hoping they're finding
That one love
Who says I'm lost in Love
Because you've got the best of my love
And I just can't stop loving you

My my my
I love your smile
Love is real
It touches and moves
It grooves
It says let me love you down
Because you loved me
At your best you are loved
Because that's the way love goes
On loves train

Let the record spin
They're playing my song
It's all about love and
The DJ got us falling in love again
Can you feel the love tonight
But let's slow down
Because love is an easy lover
And you can't hurry love

Love me
I'll be your someone to love and
I will always love you
This is no ordinary love
Our love will stand the test of time
It's like when a man loves a woman
She doesn't have to say
Love should have brought you home last night
Because love will keep us together

What the world needs now is love sweet love

If it could spread itself it would
But it needs you and me to participate
To show it
To receive it
To be it
To live it
To love it
Love is the only thing that there's just too little of
So spread love

To My Beautiful
Daughters

For Alyvia and Ava

I can't explain the joy I feel
When I look into your eyes
Just to watch you grow is a precious gift
I'm blessed with as each day goes by

To see the you that you already are
Develop more fully right before my eyes
Your smile, your quirks, the expressions you make
Your loving hugs, even the sound of your cry

The little things that make you you
That no one else possesses
All make me more in love with you
And appreciate your presence

To watch how much you grow and change
As every year goes by
Sometimes I stare as you are sleeping
Because I'm so in awe that you're mine

For God to love me enough
To allow me to be your mother
I realize the magnitude of responsibility I have
Of raising my beautiful daughters

I don't take my task lightly
Of preparing you to be a queen
Right now you're my little princesses
But one day it'll be your time to reign

I don't doubt that you'll be ready
To step into your role
Because I see it already happening
Each day as I watch you grow

_To My_
Son

Although you never graced my womb
And on the day you were born, I wasn't in the room
Didn't know to applaud when you took your first step
Couldn't ooh and ahhh when you said your first word

The first part of your life didn't include me
I wasn't there to be able to see
I didn't know you. You didn't know me
But, today that's changed and life is more complete

I always wanted to have a son
Just didn't expect that my son would already be born
And that I would have to play catch up to get to know
you
But every moment leading to you has been worth going
through

And I can't wait to see who you're going to be
To watch you grow up is one of God's sweet treats

College, marriage, career, your whole life to go
Just know I'm always praying that success will be yours

And I find it amusing how much alike you and I are
Our thoughts and our views are similar at heart
I will treasure every moment that we get to share
You'll never know the depths of how much I really care

My heart melts every time you call me mom
And I am always proud to brag about my handsome son
You are respectful, loving, even-keeled, exceedingly smart
But I most admire watching you chase God's heart

So never doubt if my intentions are real
My love and support are sincere and come from how I feel
I love you, son. You are the apple of my eye
And I'll feel that way about you until the day I die

I never carried you in my womb
On the day you were born, I wasn't in the room
I couldn't be there from the start
But for the rest of my life, I'll always carry you in my
heart

He ain't
Going Back

Let me break it down
So it can forever and consistently
Be broke

People keep trying to send Christ back to the Cross
To forgive them for their new sins
But believe me baby,
He ain't going back there again

What's done is done and all that was done
Cannot and will not be repeated
So when you're begging Christ for forgiveness,
He's at the right hand of God seated

He's probably saying
You're asking me to do what I've already done
I died for sins you did back then, are doing right now
And ones you have not yet begun

I knew that you would never be perfect
So I took your unsinned sins,
Upon my faultless shoulders
And kept them with me until the end

It was right there on Calvary
That everything was complete
Stop punishing yourself
The debt ended with me

You are a spirit dwelling in flesh
So I see beyond your sinful actions
The heart is more my focal point
Focusing on sin is a mere distraction

So when you ask me to forgive you
My child, that's already been done
My love for you is beyond sin
So change your focus to goodness of the Son

Just thank Me for the one time pardon,
exoneration, absolve, forgive
The power of the blood I shed will last
Beyond all of your years

Now go and find the joy that only comes
In the gift that new creations get
Spread the word of my goodness
To all who seem to not know or forget

Tell them:
Let me break it down
So it can forever and consistently
Be broke

People keep trying to send Christ back to the
Cross
But believe me baby,
He ain't going back there no more

L-O-V-E

Loving that you're loving me
Loving you loving us

Open up your heart, your mind,
Your soul with trust

Validate the things I do, I say,
I feel

Everything I do, I do for us
Is real

You and Me

We were born four days apart
Downtown, at Wishard Hospital
Maybe we were in the baby room together
But goo-goo and ga-ga was all we could dribble

We lived only a few blocks apart
Swam in the same pool, went to the same park
Maybe we bumped shoulders at the playground
But were much too young to feel a spark

In college I cheered at the game you scored big in
But you played for the other team
Maybe when running down field, you glanced at me
And said, "Wow, she looks like the girl for me."

I lived in Atlanta and then LA
But at different times than you
Maybe we needed a little time to mature
Before fate would have us rendezvous

Who would have thought while in St. Louis
As I walked across the space
That I'd run into my future husband
When we finally came face-to-face

That our paths would finally intersect
When you introduced yourself with a smile
We parted ways not knowing
That meeting would be so worthwhile

From there the rest is history
We're married with a family
Maybe we drew close intuitively
Because we were always meant to be

In Love

I am in Love
And so wrapped inside your intoxicating presence
I can smell the aroma of your sweet love
When you caress my 5'4 essence

Transported by sweet satisfaction
Making me high and I won't come down
Just floating on this love cloud
Enjoying the in love sound

Can't you feel my heart beating
To the vibe of our love song
Pacing itself between interludes of
A melody that plays all night long

Your love is in my love
And I swear it feels just so
It's like your lust and my lust grew up
And now our love is like whoa!

I am in Love
And I feel it when you look into my eyes
It's the touch-less touch that reaches deep
And sets the tone for the ride

You're here and I'm here
Flesh, Spirit, Soul
Two bodies oh so near
But all I see is one

Shadows projecting You-me-we
Across the room on the wall
We're a Romantic movie
With sound effects and all

Your love is in my love
And I swear it feels just so
It's like your lust and my lust grew up
And now our love is like whoa!

Beating The Struggle

Infatuation, power struggle, a choice to love
Infatuation, power struggle, a choice to love

Uncle Cleotis always says
The infatuation stage lasts an average of 2 years

I don't quite remember us making it that long
The struggle came fast, unpleasant and strong
I didn't think we were gonna last for long
Two Aries with equally hard heads
I thought I knew and you thought you knew
But neither of us really knew the truth

See unless you submit you're stuck in the power quarrel
Where I'm right and you're wrong in a non-stop struggle
Where our feelings stay hurt
And emotions control the way
I don't want to leave, but I don't want to stay

Something has to give
We can't go on this way

How can I choose love when sometimes there's emotional
pain
How can I choose love when I don't always get my way
How can I choose love when I see all your flaws shine
How can I choose love when I know you're looking at
mine

But I must choose if we plan to merge
Choosing love is the only way to purge
But it's not an easy thing for one to do
Because choosing love means
I'm not choosing me
And you're not choosing you

Don't give up on
Love

Don't give up on Love
And Love won't give up on you

Even if you have been
Disappointed
Mistreated
Abused
Damaged
All in the name of love

Don't stop believing in love
Know that you deserve love
But not
False love
Pretend love
Convenient love
Confused love

Trust God and you will find
Ride or die love
Authentic love

Cain't stop love
Won't stop love
I didn't know this could be love

You know you want to encounter love
Stand up for love
Believe in love
Be strong in love
Belong to love

Don't give up on Love
Because Love won't give up on you

I Love Me some Me

Yeah, I tell myself that I'm Fine
And I read the word to renew my mind
I treat myself to fine foods for dine
Because I love me some me

Now, I'm not perfect by no means
I might not be the girl of your dreams
But, when I look in the mirror, I see a queen
See, I love me some me

I make mistakes every now and then
I'm still a saint, even though I've sinned
I thank God for his grace, then make amends
Because I love me some me

And even if no one else will
I don't fuss, or make a big deal
I simply tell me how I feel
I say, "I love me some me"

My Mother

My beautiful mother is not a perfect woman
But she taught my sisters and I perfectly
How to love one another

My sisters and I,
We argued
We fought
We teased
Like most siblings do

After a dispute among us girls,
She would say,
"Now apologize and tell her you love her"
We didn't always like that

But, we obeyed.
We said,
"I'm sorry. I love you,"
Crying

Reluctant
Fuming
Annoyed

As much as we hated it,
It made us close
It made us better able to forgive
It made us better able to admit our wrongs
It made us better able to love

I hope I can share that same gift
With my own little girls
And my son
And maybe one day they'll say

My beautiful mother is not a perfect woman
But she taught us perfectly
How to love one another

Let There Be
Love

Since the greatest among Faith, Hope and Love
is Love
Then, that's why it had to be declared
Let There Be Love!

Let there be Love
Where love wouldn't seem to be
In the places our eyes dare not see

Let there be love
In the spots good folk don't go

Let there be love
For the friend and foe

Let there be love
For those you look at in disgust
And for those you know you could never really trust

Let there be love
For the Criminal and the Victim
For the Saint and the Sinner
For the Losers and the Winners

Let there be love
For the Abuser and the Abused
Let there be love
For the User and the Used

Let there be love
For the people you can't stand
Let there be love
For the triflin' cheatin' man

Let there be love to cover everybody's wrongs
Let there be love to forgive the things I shouldn't have done
Let there be love for the despicable, low-down, dirty crook
Let there be love for the misguided, confused, and over-looked

Let there be love for mothers and fathers who weren't
there
Let there be love for those who don't know how to care
Let there be love for the physically, mentally, and psycho-
logically ill
Let there be love even for those who have killed

A call for this kind of
Unconditional love
Would be tremendously challenging for you and me
But Christ showed that this kind of love could actually be
When he died for us on Calvary

Refreshed &
Renewed

Dedicated to My Wonderful Husband
As We Celebrate 10 Years of Holy Matrimony

Refreshed & Renewed
That's what our love is
Through
Good times and
Challenging times
Clear times or
Dim times
Our love is solid because
It's anchored to the Rock

It's not that it wasn't real
When we first started out
But under this new covenant
It has grown into something
That is sweet and cultivated
And assuring to the heart

We're connected through the old us
More in love with the new us
As we embark on our future life together
I am so confident about what we can be

I believe in who we are
I look forward to what we will do

I'll put my hand in yours
Lay my head on your shoulder
And we'll let God lead the way
With him guiding us
You know we'll be good
We can rest while we work
To make our love complete
Not faultless
Just timeless

We can call our future by name
And we call it
God ordained
Gracious
Stable
Steadfast
Fortunate
Fulfilled
Fun
Prosperous
Passionate
Caring
Committed
Blessed
Beautiful
Adoring
Abundant

I know I'm in love with all of you
I know you're in love with all of me
We roll with the good
Use His word to transform the bad
Ours is the substance that legacies are made of
It's the evolution of you and me
It's our now love
Our real love
Our future love
Refreshed and renewed

About
Tajuana TJ Butler-Jackson

Tajuana "TJ" Butler-Jackson at age 26 founded Lavelle Publishing in 1997 with the release of *The Desires of A Woman: Poems Celebrating Womanhood.* Lavelle Publishing released *Sorority Sisters* in 1998. Villard Books, a division of Random House released *Sorority Sisters,* in May 2000, which sold over 80,000 copies. Mrs. Butler-Jackson has since authored the Number One Essence Magazine Bestseller, *Hand-me-down Heartache, The Night Before Thirty,* and *Just My Luck,* all released by various divisions of Random House. Tajuana has also completed collections of poetry, including *In Love: Poems Celebrating the Essence of Love* and *Possibilities,* as part of the Lavelle Publishing Gold Series.

Tajuana has toured to various colleges and universities, conferences, and bookstores and has been interviewed by various radio and television talk show hosts throughout the U.S. Her stops have included the Essence Festival, all four NPHC Sorority Conventions, The National Black Arts Festival, Congressional Black Caucus, and the Black MBA Conference. She has spoken for the American Business Women's Association in Atlanta and the Alpha Kappa

Alpha International Regional Conference. She has also spoken or conducted workshops at the University of Maryland-College Park, Columbia University, Clark Atlanta University, Mississippi State and Florida A&M University, to name a few. Mrs. Butler-Jackson and her books have been featured in Essence Magazine, Upscale, Today's Black Woman, Honey Magazine, NV Business Magazine, Black Issues Book Review, Black Book Review and Publisher's Weekly.

TJ launched Butlertown Productions, an organization that produces via a variety of mediums, in 2005. Butlertown's projects have included the *Tajuana "TJ" Butler Sisterhood Cruise* 2005. The cruise departed Miami, Florida and cruised to Nassau, Bahamas August 5-8th; short films, *Discovered* and *Inside Perspective*; *Hand-me-down Heartache The Musical*, which played May and September 2012 in Indianapolis, Indiana; the unreleased *Hand-me-down Heartache Music CD*; and the *No More Excuses: Black Men Stand Up! Conference* for men and young men, every May with husband, Nationally Renowned Speaker and Author, Robert Jackson.

Butler currently resides in Indianapolis with her husband and their children Ava Simone, Alyvia Rae and Robert Tye.

www.tjbutler.com

Other Books from
Lavelle Publishing

The No More Excuses Curriculum
by Robert Jackson:
  Black Men Stand Up!
  The Workbook: A Boy's Guide to Manhood
  Solutions to Educating Black & Latino Males
  Put a Stop to Bullying
  The Workbook for Girls: A Girl's Guide to Womanhood

Coldness in July by Carolyn Spencer

Lavelle Publishing
Gold Series

The Lavelle Publishing Gold Series is a series of books that are printed with the utmost attention to detail. Each copy will also be hand signed by the author on the Half-Title Page. Be assured that if you have purchased this book or received it as a gift, your very special book is a valuable keepsake to be treasured for years to come. Please look for other Gold Series Poetry Books by Tajuana "TJ" Butler-Jackson.